Published by Sohini Dasgupta
on behalf of Lime n Limpid
www.limenlimpid.com

Under the Copyright Act of India, 1957

Edition 1 - 2024

One of these days

Sreya Dutt

Illustrations by

Partha P Mitra

We wish to express our gratitude to all our friends and well – wishers, who have been a tremendous source of support and encouragement.

This book is a result of imagination, self-introspection, observation and inspiration.

Contents

Green

Every time of the year, every year there are plenty of surprises in store, we just have to look. The charmed days of winter are gone, and they bring with them a season of restlessness and waiting. It can be a rather doomed wait as it only promises never-ending sultry days. When there's a strange fear, of losing everything as things seem poised on this precipice, about to fall into some awful degradation. And the heat into which we were born, the burden we must bear all our lives makes a comeback into our lives, and we accept its terror with that old familiar resignation, tied as we are to its tyranny for life. Winter seems like a long-lost dream, a stranger.

And yet when you look out of the window and you see the black bareness that rudely thrusts itself out into the blue everyday replaced by a riot of young, tiny, green growths, you do feel a little thrill. The journey of discovering it again anew, and it never ceases to surprise. All the green freshness as it proliferates every day until the green and blue meet.

And that makes you feel a little reassured, to see the old cycle begin anew, and colour flood the sky. The movement of life and its appearance is always delicate, always beautiful.

And you can't help but ask in the same breath, softly, in an inaudible whisper, "Where's my colour?"

Winter

Warm, mellow sunshine that illuminates everything around, casting a glow of dreamy contentment.

Sunlight that falls on a staircase through the unwashed glass, lighting up those faces and footsteps that scurry or trudge along it every day, lending them character all of a sudden.

A shower of cascading tiny yellow leaves descending from above, caught in the path of so many beams of sun. Soft sun, playing on faces and smiles.

Early winter haze dispelled by the penetrating warmth.

Oranges. Soaking in the smells of winter, a citrusy warmth which you feel like revisiting anew every day.

A quiet air of celebration ringing in the air, ushered in by the sun. Warmth all around, as worries and work seem to fade far away and dissolve in lazy afternoons spent in soaking it all in, and basking in this newfound glory.

Days that seem charmed, with the wish to grasp this sun and hold it forever.

Movements

At times you feel tired of waiting, in suspension. Coiled like a spring, waiting for the leaf to fall, the cloud to move, the breeze to flutter. You watch beautiful fluid bodies, gliding across the stage, agents - guiding action. But then, who is guiding them, you pause to ask. You're that sceptical of motion? Sometimes you just wish and wish things happened to you with a bang, a dramatic lightning burst of inspired movement. You're taught to be static - ask, question, interrogate ... it should all be cerebral. But you feel all tired and lost. You want action. Freedom. Tired of running after bids at action, you simply want things to happen to you.

Motion is so seductive.

And yet in the mass of bodies milling around madly, you want to be separate. Distant. Stand apart. Gaze at the chaos in serene isolation.

What do you want?

And here we are again

Today's a nice day, it could be any other day, but it feels like a day in its own right ... a day to hold on to and then a day to let go of ... let loose into the days gone ... that's the way days are ... right now, it seems so nice to hold on tight to today and hope it doesn't end...But of course, it will, and that's why today is worth soaking in completely ... this windy blustery day with grey skies and yes the familiar vista from the window and the green which seems dense, opaque and endless and the incessant buzz of machinery that you learn to ignore... tends to disturb these moments of tranquil contemplation but there's nothing to be done, they must be woven in as well... because otherwise, today won't be today, it would be any other day. And the smell of fish that's still on my fingers ... an unforgettable smell that we'll have to bid goodbye to in a while... all the sounds and smells, all of which will come again and revisit us anew...

But there still won't be a day like today.

Blood on the sand

Ciudad Juarez. It's far away from where I stay. Ciudad Juarez. It's a border town far, far, away. Ciudad Juarez is thousands of miles away. There are people in Ciudad Juarez. People I don't know. People I don't see. People I will never meet. Yet I know of the people in Ciudad Juarez. I know of little girls who work there. I have heard of *maquiladoras*. I have heard that they have long, black hair and silent faces. I have heard that they work for hours on end. I believe their fingers are skilled and dextrous and they are experts at assemblage. I know their work is good stuff. I know their fingers are carried across the border, across the Rio Grande. I know they dream of crossing. Their lives are searches for dreams. They come to Ciudad Juarez to find those dreams. I've been told Ciudad Juarez only allures. Juarez entices.

It's the land that pulls at them - the tiny, tiny birds. They fly to Ciudad Juarez from plateau, hill, and valley. They fly away from sadness and the struggle back home. I've been told Ciudad Juarez isn't very nice. I've been told it's of the black sort. It apparently doesn't treat them very nice. Their dreams begin to fade. And the colours begin to get lost in the darkness. I've been told their lives are no fun. And yet people do want to have *them* for fun. So, they do. I've been told it goes on quite regularly. I've been told it happens a lot. And the figures are high. As their hopes crash and fall, the figures whoopee in delight. They take turns and twists. They are climbing high.

Ciudad Juarez is a monster. It swallows them whole. But there are far too many to be sampled. So, what if all of them have long black hair? The monotony is secondary. Ciudad Juarez plays the number game with wicked abandon. It has records to break. And statistics to spell anew. So, they all land up in the desert. I've been told no one can hear. And as the sands creep up, eating into their prey, Ciudad Juarez grows more and more magnificent. Larger. Mightier. All glory.

There is blood on the sand. Scavengers always feast on the borders of Ciudad Juarez. In Juarez, the borders between life and death are dissolving. There is blood on the sand. Ciudad spits out all that long, black, straight hair. What a waste. Their souls are lost. Take back all that hair, Juarez.

Take it back to your factories. Put it to use. And ship it back. There is blood on the sand. There has been blood on the sand. Juarez can't see. I can. It can't be wiped away. The desert winds can't erode it away to oblivion. Cannot. Long black hair and cries as terrible as the howling winds. Moans that I can hear here.

Can't you Juarez?

They lie in wait. Monster, beware.

Once again

Rather nondescript, must be reached trailing buzzing flies that are not even flicked aside casually. Malodorous place, tiny. "Licence done here", the printout shows flashy cars! That's what's new. Exploding with neatly stacked colours and women who argue, elaborate, explain, nitpick as they try to flatter themselves to the patient smiling personages who listen, and listen some more. They let on a lot of themselves here, it seems. Their shapes and their lives as well. Their demands are quite tiresome in the cramped heat and the phone keeps ringing, crowding the space with more women's harried voices and the same patient drawl attends to them, as the voices keep breaking in, nagging, insistent, repetitive, harried, bordering on the verge of hysteria. And opposite is the place of worship. An old man peeked down from the workshop above. Bespectacled and white-bearded. Stinging mosquitoes. Thriving business. And yet there's a muted sense of excitement for me because I feel like an outsider and yet I like to imagine things here. I like to think of this place beyond the women, the listening, the phone, the flies, mosquitoes. I like to keep looking and smiling within. Like believing that I was born to be absurd and think of unlikely things. Feel like abandoning myself here mentally, though outwardly I'm always composed. Float far way and feel myself go, and step outside my proper self. It doesn't surprise me that this place has inspired lyricism in me, however muted. Beauty doesn't inspire beauty. The residues remain etched in my mind as we travel through the heat. And they always will. The tableau is very vast and there's always the scope of adopting a panoramic vision, leading a life of impossibilities. But the reality is toned down, innocuous, circumspect, and hesitant.

More movements

We all have our little pretensions and sharp steely bits of pride. Like brandishing them now and then, to reinforce our definitions of ourselves. We shape ourselves in so many respects, pitting ourselves against so many isolated opposites. Constantly fighting against those definitions, consciously, or otherwise. Adjustments are hard, and difficult to believe in.

And when your armour cracks, and all the training, from the self and other informed quarters disintegrates with a crash, you feel the darkness. Dams break, and water gushes to the hard, icy, desert depths of denial. You're flooded with the power of a force you can't really reckon with. It inundates you, filling you to the core completely. You're submerged neck-deep, lost in yourself. And as you wander lost, blindfolded, dismayed, betrayed you wake up to the shock of discovery- it hits you very hard. You've been silently attacked. And you ask yourself, like you did the time before, "Do I want to surrender?" And the answer is always, and you know it, it always is a resounding 'Yes.'

And with that 'Yes' you know you can dance the spirals of gay freedom, silhouetted against the fading shadows of victory.

You feel the lightness of fleet-footed crazy freedom, echoing against the laughter of your liberated soul.

And as you move towards yourself and delve deep into yourself, you feel refreshed, because you have also moved away.

You feel the salt tang of freshness and you drink it with feverish pleasure, because you know it's yours. You just want to make it your own.

These little secret gasps of freedom you yearn for, and they come to you in the most startling of ways, colouring your world with the hues of sunsets, snatches of brilliant blue sky and also the dark, threatening, cloud-laden sky, pregnant with hope and rain.

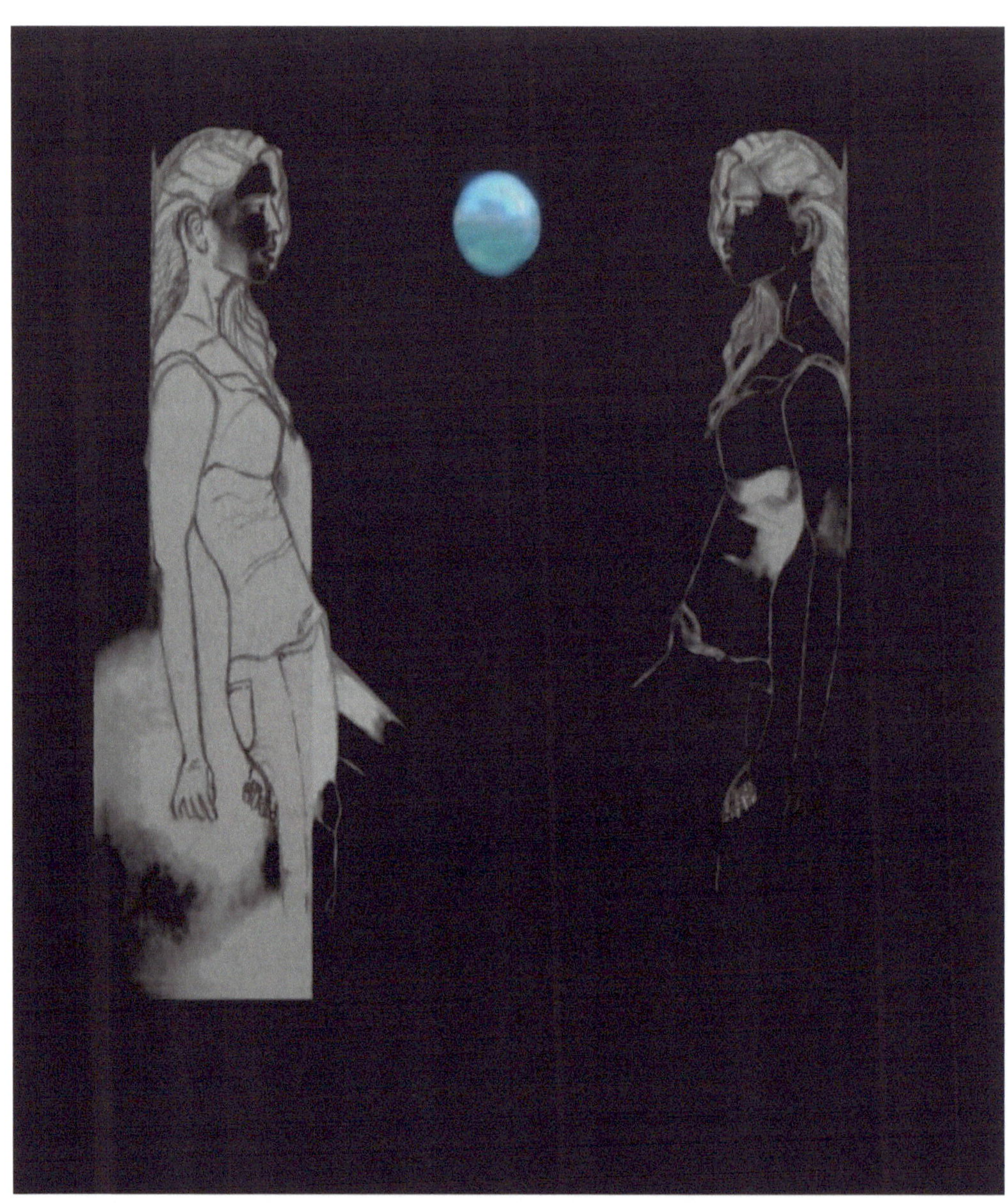

White

They pop up at you all the time, a veritable assault of milky women, blazing in a glory of blinding 'white.' There's this actress who grins, flashing her teeth and her skinny legs and her dog on which she is shown to shower all the affection that she couldn't perhaps summon for her on-screen lovers. She's content with his spots, they must flourish, how else would he be the canine privileged enough to merit her caresses? But for herself, she must avail of a magic potion, because she must be blemish-free. She triumphantly flashes it, that yellow vial promising perfection.

And there are others who enjoy fairy tale turnarounds, from being dark, neglected women spurned at every avenue, wallowing in the 'darkness' of rejection. A matter of weeks, and they are blessed with whiteness and suddenly, the world is at their feet, they need not even stoop to conquer. Dazzlingly they smile, flooding the world with radiant fairness and the jingle takes an effervescent, upward turn, telling us of the right fairness of it all, how these poor women have reached the end of a trajectory of 'struggle' that promises only light, and more light. Men gaze flabbergasted at that shy, cowering creature and her transformation, mesmerised in open-mouthed admiration, their jaws on the verge of unhinging, at the perfect mate, a fantasy of white materialised - delightful, delectable prospect!

The path-breaking first cream, in that unmistakable tube of pink and white, has undergone many avatars and become metonymic in our national consciousness for the fairness formula. Of late, we see a perky actress who enters a laboratory, demanding with zest the perfect solution for the perfect fairness. And she bounces out with glee, all darkness, taint, and blemish vanished, shooting forth an aura of whiteness that encapsulates her entirely - it could blind the sun in its intensity.

And there is another, playfully fooling around with her lover, unstrapping that strap and revelling in glory at the benign protection provided by her cream, the faithful shield that grants her uninterrupted fairness. Chuckling in victory over the defeated man, who can vouch for no such 'protective guardian' she returns to his embrace.

And so many more, super hulks and screen gods who say that they swear by fairness, men too have found their calling.

In discussions, some are up in arms, some laugh, some practice indifference - it is the way advertising works, you must understand they say, it is a national obsession and must be cashed in upon- look at the business it has spawned. And so, rolls the juggernaut, spinning fantasies for women that are consumed voraciously, in all 'fairness,' it's only 'fair' that women should want a 'fair' taste of 'fairness.'

Dreary

It's one of those terrible days again when you know that something is amiss, of feeling completely out-of-sync with the cosmos and its ordered chaos. It's a nagging sense of worry that you just can't pin down, yet it continues to gnaw at your insides feasting on all happiness until you seem to be a weakened and pulverised shadow soul, a husk of emptiness.

How it gnaws, with such insistence.

And the worst fears come to the surface, all those fears - they come with such marching confidence. Swirling miasma of fear that forces sharp intakes of breadth. Blinding sun, no longer benign.

Confined to these thoughts, and enslaved to them forever. Aching for lightness.

When nothing seems attractive, even fantasies become empty.

Frozen

The other evening, I was returning from another orgy of stupidity and banality. At the crossing, the auto halted at the traffic signal. It had been a sweltering hot day. I looked out of the window to my right and my breath froze for a second. It's a sight I love witnessing time and again. The street lights on that side of the road were defunct for some reason, and that bit was a little less lit. And there weren't too many people around either. It was a white polythene bag, the cheap less than 30 microns ones. It was fluttering about, lifted up and put down again by the breeze. It seemed like the world had gone 'hush' for a moment, frozen into immobility and silence. I watched its movements and it brought to mind something almost identical I'd seen some years ago. But that had been right in front, playing at the base of my feet. This was a spectacle viewed from afar.

And the auto started off again.

White polythene bags and their little solo dances. Solitude in motion, of the celebratory sort. It really is one of the most beautiful things.

Dream

It was the same place with the same people where you grew up. And yet different, morphed out of a film, with snazzy, glossy and officious details. It was the same enduring crush and the nagging threat of being rejected and meeting that rejection with the same sense of shattering. And the same friend who got pulled into a gadget. And venturing out to grapple with being essentially alone. Stepping out from the so-called seat of learning into the mecca of consumerism, a place we all inhabit with wide-eyed wonder. And shockingly, I saw her, a figure from the past, derided, ridiculed, jeered at, lonely, and at that point of my life, from where I knew her, also a lot like me. She was sitting on the floor, looking beautiful, dazzlingly so - a picture of cool serenity, chained at the neck to a tall pillar. I was stumped and I wanted to know why. I ventured further and realised myself to be the subject of the stentorian, brisk, efficient teacher figure's gaze. She was looking at me with displeasure and disapproval that sent waves of rejection of another sort in my direction, she was with a stern-faced companion I didn't know. No, I wasn't here for an exam, I didn't want to appear for it either I explained, as their lips curled. I just want to know why she's chained. And I want to talk to her. I felt a pressing need to talk to her. And so, they took me there. Why are you like this? She didn't reply. They showed me an album, with many pretty pictures of her, and recalling how she had faced taunts for being stupid, out-of-place, and plain out of her mind, I said, "Why not take a turn to fashion?"

And then suddenly, before I knew it, I was on the ground, her impassive face was crowding into mine, and I was being shaken, shaken, shaken. My world was shaking and more than the pain it was the rejection that left me stupefied, stunned, shocked and gasping for survival.

And the stentorian figures stood erect, a little distance away, watching with calm indifference, a naturalist gaze…

Scratching the surface

The dark red brick building loomed ahead of them as they slowly and silently walked towards it. Their heads were bowed and they shuffled their feet, staring at each other uneasily and looking over their shoulders. The weather was playing its part in unsettling them even further - the oppressive leaden grey sky hung over them, seemingly swallowing them with its proximity. The cold, biting winds slashed them across their faces and it seemed to Ilya that the winds wanted to mark them as doomed, brand them as losers walking towards inevitable defeat. It was difficult to raise his head to look at the girl next to him, but Ilya dared to. Yes, they were condemned to face their fates alone, but this silent march made Ilya think of a brief companionship - a sense of togetherness before that final blow, a few moments of shared silence. He was unaware of what she was thinking but he began the inward journey into his thoughts just as the walk entered the final lap. He felt chilled to his heart but still kept up the struggle to etch the lines of his imagined world.

Here and now

It's good to be silly. It's good to giggle. It's good to say absurd, illogical and nonsensical stuff - you end up sponsoring a few laughs and a couple of incredulous looks. It's good to look for bright, shiny objects that may be quite cheap but it's good to be dazzled by them. It's good to stare out of the window into blocks of concrete and imagine oneself being transported, many miles away. It's good to watch sparrows taking dust baths or hopping about or chirping away in their usual fashion. It's good to watch inane soap operas and follow their slow narratives. It's good to have shared happiness and stock jokes that are reiterated endlessly. It's good to laugh together and laugh over memories of shared laughs. It's good to be free, good to feel free and hope it all lasts forever.

Fever

Fever came calling after so many days.

No, it wasn't a fevered wait. No anticipation, no longing.

Welcome you with an old familiarity. Glad you came after so long. Feels like having a constant companion. Someone who understands life's innate burdens and yet gives you the gift of lightness.

Being fevered is also being gifted with lightness, as all other heavy things evaporate away while you cling to this old companion in an embrace of complicity.

Open

Was trying to figure out why storms are never old, and why everything about them is always breathtaking, always spelling relief.

Thank God for storms.

Very few parts of the world enjoy the privilege of participating in that process of slowly built anticipation that is so eternal, so timeless.

And all the songs of yearning we have, of a woman aching for her lover whose skin is as dark-hued as the rain-bearing clouds, can perhaps approximate what that means, the promise.

Love storms for another reason - as the skies are ripped apart and mad gusts of wind shake trees, tossing, and twisting in a frenzy, we are afforded a chance to see our internal turbulence(s) played out in the open quite spectacularly.

And our tired lives hinging on nothingness and everyday hells become dramatic and compelling, making us gasp, arresting the monotony for a brief flash of illumination. Our inward struggles and worries, so clamping, clinging, cloying and wearisome become the stuff of legend as we try to transcend the disgust we feel every day, choking on spit and tears we're too polite to spill out, too tortured to see manifest.

And staring awestruck at the sky, as it changes hues, exposing ourselves to something infinitely grander, and liberating, we want to forget everything else.

Makes us feel heroic, imagining ourselves to be part of this greater unleashing of primal forces.